I0149889

Sista, Watch for the Hook!

OBSERVATIONS OF HUMANITY VOL.1

BY DASH'E

www.squarepennypress.com

CONTENTS

DEDICATION

There are so many individuals who have contributed to this work of art, unknowingly and knowingly. First, I want to thank my grandmother: Ms. Bettie R. Young. I thank her for her continuous love on this earth plane as well as in the ethers. The love between you and me is eternal.

I want to thank my grandfather who helped raise me in his way, paying the local women of the neighborhood $0.50 to change my diaper (lol).

On an educational and life journey note, I want to thank:

- Ms. Deborah Cooper: *www.survivingdating.com*
- The Honor Family: *www.lenonhonor.com*
- Dr. Joy Degruy
- Ms. Fluebrun
- K.P.
- Tom Burrell - author of the book *Brainwashed: Challenging the Myth of Black Inferiority*
- Ms. Savage
- The Hewitts
- Ms. Gail

- Mo'Nique and Sidney Hicks - *Mo'Nique and Sidney's Open Relationships Podcast*
- Mr. Bell (the best art teacher in the world and a lover of biscuits)

I also want to thank humanity. It was through our interactions I was able to put in place a book that would call attention to solutions that would help us when interacting with one another.

Last, but certainly not least, I want to thank Tiffany and Kanise and the team at Square Penny Publishing and Writeportunity. Both of you have helped in activating and implementing this work of art into this reality and for that, I thank you.

Activating Highest Good Only.

1 Luv,

- DaSh'e

"To embrace new worlds,

you have to embrace new ideas."

Dr. Phlox, Star Trek

WHO IS DASH'E?

There is a saying: you have a day you are born, a day that you transition, and in between, there is a dash. So, for me, I am working on my dash in life. Hence, the name DaSh'e. You may encounter my musings and think, *this sista's flow is unique!* Well, you would be right! DaSh'e loves to get messages across with a dose of humor and a bit of music. For example, DaSh'e loves the song and message behind the song "Level Up" by Ciara.

DaSh'e firmly believes that one day someone is going to use the song "Level Up" for their praise dance song selection in church. Nah, I'm just messin'. But no really, in my opinion, the "Level Up" song by Ciara is a summoning call to the Divine Feminine, letting the ladies know it is time to emerge. Even when you break down the words "level up," to me, it's saying, "Eve Up." That has a special meaning for us, my sistas, because in my opinion, Eve has been spoken so ill of – especially in certain church circles. I feel that one of the effects of this type of teaching of making Eve at fault is used as justification for emotional, mental, and yes — sometimes even physical abuse towards women. So, now that Ciara has presented us with this song, I feel that it is one of MANY signs of the awakening for the Divine Feminine. We are UP, and we are rising. The time is now.

So, as you open your mind and peruse these pages, you may wonder if DaSh'e's observations are for you. Well, to go more in depth of who the writings of DaSh'e may represent, they are for those who are looking for a different perspective. DaSh'e seeks also to provide an "aha" moment for that young sista who is struggling to deal. These sistas are not *watchful* for the hook that lures them further away from their Divine Feminine.

This is also for the sista who has gone through life experiences that had once stifled the growth of her inner child, but now she is ready to move forward. The writings of DaSh'e are also for sistas who have friendships with women of different cultures who may want to address underlying issues to make sure the friendship is built on a firm foundation. There are no limitations to the *Observations of DaSh'e*. They can be applied in the workplace and in organizations that are truly "about that life" of diversity and truly believe that there is strength in diversity. The writings of DaSh'e are great for group discussions and intellectual get togethers, as well as for stimulating pillow talks.

DaSh'e's *Random Thoughts on The Power of Music*: the older I get, the more I get "in tune" with the lyrics of a song – not just the beat. For me, the lyrics of each of these songs are filled with diamond jewels for those who are willing to dig for the deeper meaning. Cause face it, there's always a deeper meaning.

Here's the playlist:

1. "Just Do You" - India Arie

2. "Window Seat (monologue)" - Erkyah Badu

3. "I am Not My Hair" - India Arie

4. "A Rose Is Still A Rose" - Aretha Franklin

5. "Keep Tryin"- Groove Theory

6. "Closer" - Goapele

7. "Alright" - CeCe Winans

8. "Maybe God Trying to Tell You Something" - TaTa Vega

9. "Female Energy" - Willow Smith

10. "When Am I Going to Make A Living" - Sade

11. "Woman" - Raheem DeVaughn

12. "Tribute to a Woman"- Ginuwine

13. "It's Your World (Pop's spoken word part)"- Common

So, let us begin. You got this, Sis!

-DaSh'e

WHAT DOES "WATCH FOR THE HOOK" MEAN?

Watch for the hook. Interesting title, right? Well, it has significance. See, back in the day, they had this song by a rap artist named Cool Breeze. It featured the group OutKast and another group called Goodie Mob. It should be noted that Cool Breeze was a fine brotha, too. (I don't know why I felt the need to put that in there, but I did.) Anyway, the hook of the song went like this:

See what you need to do is learn the tricks of the trade

Go to work, put it down, and den get paid

You betta listen to your corner and watch for The hook

Those lyrics of the song really stuck out to me, especially when I first heard them in '97. Now, 20-plus years later, as I write this, I finally can grasp the meaning of the lyrics instead of just nodding my head to the beat. Now, don't get me wrong: I can understand why some people would think mentioning that song is an oxymoron. However, there's nothing wrong with a little remix. DaSh'e views the feminine as one of MANY gifts of being a woman. What gifts do you ask? Well, please: let me elaborate.

The gift of going within oneself.

The gift of being IN-tuned.

But sista, we have to ACTivate that gift! You have to be on the lookout! You have to see with more than your eyes and watch with your ears to the sly accusations around us – these alien phrases that try to weigh us down. Sista we must be mindful and listen. There is something very receptive about the act of listening. But do not be passive! Oh no! Let us absorb and engage on a higher level. Let us *watch for it and listen*. Hence the name **Sista, Watch for The Hook.**

This book is a form of therapy for me. It also derives from a deep passion to get alot of things off my chest – a passion to get an important message out that needs to be heard – a message that needs to get to the next generation. For too long, there have been too many left hooks that have been thrown at sistas. Yet, society acts like sistas are just supposed to take it without saying a word. When we do react, however, and sistas say something, society boxes us in with phrases and labels such as "angry black woman" to try to keep us quiet. So sistas, when I say, "watch for the hook," I mean it. You don't have to allow the hook to connect; you can bob that mug (like Big Momma said in the movie *Soul Food:* "Strike a might ttt eee blow"). All jokes aside – sistas: let's gon' head and strike that blow. Too many hooks have been thrown.

INSECURE WHITE WOMEN

THE SET UP

Growing up, I was conditioned to believe that white women were the epitome of beauty via television programming, as well as through ignorant-ass sayings passed off as truth like: "now if a white man marry a black woman, he really loves that black woman." Ignorant issh right? I know, but that's the type of issh that's passed down in some families. So, up until the age of 33, I understood this conditioning as truth, until I realized that no amount of looking, dressing, or talking a certain way was going to change an individual's mind if her mind was already made up or if she was committed to misunderstanding you.

THE HOOK

The individuals that taught me this lesson were an anatomy instructor and this old ass white lady.

The Anatomy Instructor

I had enrolled in a well-known massage therapy school in Virginia Beach. My first class was taught by this white instructor.

During her teaching commentary, she would make references to the female gremlin of the movie "Gremlins" as well as make references to women who had big behinds and describe the way that they would walk. She would refer to the walks as "duck walks." The issue was brought to her supervisor's attention. Of course, she played the role of the "helpless, threatened, white girl" (with an added dose of crying for extra measure), while attempting to portray me as the "aggressive black lady." She denied what was happening in the classroom, even though there were others who confirmed her behavior in the classroom.

The Old Ass White Lady

I encountered this individual while walking in a local park. This old ass white lady began to have a conversation with me telling me about her life, as well as asking me questions about my life. The conversation was going well, so I had no problem with the questions she was asking me until she made the statement that I needed to lose weight because I'm fat. I told Old Ass that beauty is not owned by one culture. She then proceeded to ask me if I was married. (*Now, watch for the hook.*) I tell her my value as a woman doesn't go up or down if I'm married or not.

Now these two situations happened around the same time. It was at this point that I realized a pattern and that something had to be said about these comments.

The Observations of DaSh'e

As long as insecure white women continue to try to use sistas as a floatation device, there will continue to be covert/overt hostility between white women and sistas. It continues to be a double standard when it comes to sistas and white women when we consider looks and overall treatment.

The beauty standard myth

Let's consider looks. If a sista decides to use a perm to straighten her hair, she is automatically told: "you trying to be a WHITTTTTTTE woman (got to make sure you pronounce the T; it seems to have a better effect for some reason.).

If we continue to consider looks: if a sista decides to lighten her skin, she is told she is trying to be a white woman. However, if a white woman uses browning lotion or gets a tan, it's crickets.

Lastly, when we consider looks: if a white woman gets a perm to make her hair curly, it seems like it's even more crickets. I never hear anyone running up to her saying "You trying to be a BLACCCCCCCKKK woman."

How we're treated

If a white woman has a situation and the police are called, the following questions are asked:

1. "OMG! Are you okay?"

2. "OMG! What happened?"

Meanwhile, the sista must go through a line of questioning like:

1. "What did YOU do?"

2. "Did you roll your eyes?"

3. "Did you do any neck rolling?"

4. "Were you aggressive in any way?"

The sista: "I blinked."

The line of questioning squad: "OMG! You blinked!! See you shouldn't have blinked."

Did you see The Hook?

How do we move forward to honor the Divine Feminine?

Here are my suggestions:

1. Have an open, honest dialogue about what's going on.

2. Tell each other the things we admire about one another's culture.

3. Recognize and laugh when the media or patriarchal system tries to conquer and divide.

4. Speak up! Address the situation the moment it happens.

5. Stop being scared to speak your truth.

6. Allow individuals the space to be able to process their truth. This includes society allowing this as well.

7. As a society, we should stop trying to dismiss a sista's voice when she states how she feels.

8. Avoid terms or phrases such as: "just get over it" or "stop holding on to the past." This includes rhetorical questions that are used to antagonize as well, like: "why are y'all so angry?"

The Discussion

Melanated women and dealing with other nationalities:

1. Have you ever had an experience with other nationalities/races of women that made you feel uncomfortable?

_____

_____

_____

_____

_____

2. How did you feel?

_____

_____

_____

_____

_____

3. Did you feel heard?

_____

_____

_____

_____

4. Did you ever feel that your words were twisted?

_____

_____

_____

_____

_____

_____

5. Do you feel that the media or patriarchal system tries to create a divide between different nationalities of women? If so, why?

_____

_____

_____

_____

_____

6. Were you scared to speak your truth? In what ways?

_____

_____

_____

_____

_____

7. Do you feel society tries to dismiss what some sistas have to say when it comes to how they are treated?

_____

_____

_____

_____

_____

8. Do you feel that there are open and honest dialogues between sistas and other nationalities of women?

_____

_____

_____

_____

_____

9. What interlude/suggestions do you have?

_____

_____

_____

_____

Mantra:

Beauty is not owned by one culture.

DOUBLE STANDARD "REALITY" TV

THE SET UP

I was listening to a broadcast that was discussing how certain reality shows are making sistas look bad. I've even heard comments such as "that's why society looks down on sistas." Whelp, sorry to tell ya: this script was written loooooooooooong before "reality" shows came along. Sistas we don't have to subscribe to their script. We can write our own individual narrative that fits our own paths of happiness. Without any apologies.

THE HOOK

How sistas get judged as a collective based on the characters played on reality TV.

If sistas have a disagreement on television, they are automatically categorized as "ratchet." This is hilarious to me, because I remember on season six of a housewives show based in New York City, one of the housewives had an altercation and took her prosthetic/fake leg and threw that mug on the floor. What was even crazier was that when the camera zoomed in on the leg, even the toenail was painted. It was crazy because no one said this lady was ratchet nor was the TV show categorized as making all white women look bad.

The Observations of DaSh'e

How do we address this behavior? I think the same leeway that is given toward white shows should be applied toward black shows. How? Here are a couple of examples I personally practice:

1. When watching black reality shows, I watch them the same way I watch the "Young and the Restless" soap opera.

2. I laugh! In my mind, when I watch the basketball wives show, if I played a game of pickup basketball, I would pick the characters of Tami and Brandi to be on my team. They have some hellified defense and offense. I definitely would have Jackie on my team 'cuz she can do some hellified alley-oops and layups. If I was at a family reunion, I would want Dime and Tommie of Love and Hip Hop on my team for a game of horseshoe. They drank throw game is strooong. You have to have some strong wrist action to be able to throw drinks and hit your target. I also would have them on my team to play a game of darts. But I digress.

The Discussion

1. Do you feel that more leeway is given toward white shows?

_____

_____

_____

_____

2. Do you feel that black shows are given any leeway as far as their portrayal of black people?

_____

_____

_____

_____

_____

_____

3. If you do watch black reality shows, do you watch/see them the same way as when you watch white reality shows? What about movies?

_____

_____

_____

_____

_____

4. What about other television programming?

_____

_____

_____

_____

_____

_____

5. Do you feel that the portrayal of black people on television affects people's perceptions?

_____

_____

_____

_____

_____

_____

6. Do you feel that there is an unfair portrayal of American Blacks?

_____

_____

_____

_____

_____

7. Why do you feel this way?

_____

_____

_____

_____

8. Why do you feel that American Blacks are judged as whole rather than as individuals? Why or why not?

_____

_____

_____

_____

_____

9. What interlude/suggestions do you have to address these issues?

_____

_____

_____

_____

_____

Mantra:

I can be informed but not influenced. I define who I am.

RACE CARD / POLICE CARD / SISTAS AND THE POLICE

THE SET UP

I had a particular incident in which I had signed up for a comedy school and the instructor waited until the day before graduation to tell me that he wasn't going to "let me" graduate. When I pointed out his hidden agenda, he got frustrated and pulled the police card. What's the police card you ask? In my opinion the police card is the white people's answer to some black people's "race card." Some white people like to pull out this card when it's convenient, e.g. when they have been caught in a lie and other manipulation tactics aren't working. But anyhow back to the situation.

THE HOOK

Luckily, the responding officers saw through the instructor's bull. What was even sadder was when I told certain individuals what happened to me, I had to go through a line of questioning like this:

Me: I had a situation at the comedy school and the police were called.

Them: What! What did YOU do?

Me: Nothing

Them: Are you sure? Did you do any neck rolling? Did you roll your eyes?

Me: Yes. No. No. All I did was blink my eyes?

Them: See, see you shouldn't have blinked, and the police wouldn't have been called.

Me: Err (Scooby Doo)

What's crazy is that I do notice when it comes to white women the scenario is totally different.

White woman: OMG, I had a situation at the comedy school and the police were called.

Them: OMG, you poor thing. (Followed by hugs and kisses and cupping of their face while looking in their eyes) What happened! Are you okay! Did anyone help you?

Did you see the hook?

The Observations of DaSh'e

How do we address this behavior?

1. Don't automatically assume that the sista did something wrong.

2. Sistas deserve the same type of compassion as other races of women.

3. Sistas: you have a right to speak out when an injustice has been done to you. Don't allow society to categorize you as being aggressive, which I think is a trigger term. You have a right to be assertive.

The Discussion

1. Have you ever had a situation or experience with the "popo" or the police?

_____

_____

_____

_____

_____

_____

2. Do you feel that when some sistas have situations with the police that they receive compassion?

_____

_____

_____

_____

_____

_____

3. Do you feel that sistas are supported in the same way as brothas when it comes police brutality? How does it make you feel?

_____

_____

_____

_____

_____

4. Have you ever been ostracized for refusing to protest a situation concerning black males? How did it make you feel?

_____

_____

_____

_____

_____

5. Do you feel that there is a pressure for sistas to always come to the rescue? How does it make you feel?

_____

_____

_____

_____

_____

6. Have you ever had a situation in which you felt that the protection you provided was not reciprocated? How did it make you feel?

_____

_____

_____

_____

_____

7. Have you ever spoken out about an injustice that had been done to you? How was it received? Were you supported? How did it make you feel?

_____

_____

_____

_____

_____

8. Have you ever been accused of being aggressive? How did it make you feel?

_____

_____

_____

_____

_____

9. Do you feel the term "aggressive" is used unjustly towards sistas? How does it make you feel?

_____

_____

_____

_____

_____

_____

10. What are your suggestions?

_____

_____

_____

_____

_____

_____

Mantra:

I am safe and secure.

DANE IF YOU HAVE A MAN
DANE IF YOU DON'T

THE SET UP

I have also observed where in some parts of society, they will shame a sista especially when it comes to relationships. I've heard people say, "she will do anything or let him do anything just to say she got a man." However, I have also observed that if a sista doesn't have a man, .she is somehow looked at as though she is inadequate or something is wrong with her.

The Observations of DaSh'e

How do we address this behavior?

1. Realize everyone has his or her own unique lessons to learn when it comes to love relationships.

2. A sista's value doesn't go up or down if she has a man or not.

3. Compassion – if another sista tells of her situation that she has dealt with involving love, don't shame her

saying, "girl, you crazy, stupid, and 'fill in the blank.'" I wouldn't take that. Those type of responses create competition as well as a hierarchy.

4. These types of responses can also make a sista feel judged and cause her to shut down emotionally. I also think it is important to provide a place of confidentiality. If confidentiality is not taken into consideration, it reinforces the notion that women are not to be trusted.

The Discussion

1. Have you ever been "shamed" for not having a man, a huzzzband, being single, or not being married?

_____

_____

_____

_____

_____

2. Have you ever been "pressured" once you got married to get unmarried/divorce?

_____

_____

_____

_____

_____

3. Have you ever been shamed for still being married?

_____

_____

_____

_____

_____

4. Have you ever felt you had to keep personal romantic relationship issues to yourself even though you wanted to talk about to process the situation?

_____

_____

_____

_____

_____

5. Do you feel that the "pass down advice" of married women shouldn't be around single women is true? Why or why not?

_____

_____

_____

_____

_____

6. Has this type of advice affected your relationship with women?

_____

_____

_____

_____

_____

7. Do you feel that you have compassion when another woman discusses her romantic relationships with you?

_____

_____

_____

_____

_____

8. Do you feel single women get treated differently than married women? Why or why not?

_____

_____

_____

_____

_____

9. Have you ever compared yourself to married women? Why or why not?

_____

_____

_____

_____

_____

10. Have you ever compared yourself to single women? Why or why not?

_____

_____

_____

_____

_____

11. Do you ever feel there is a rift between single women and married women?

_____

_____

_____

_____

_____

12. What are your suggestions to help heal the rift between single and married women?

_____

_____

_____

_____

_____

Mantra:

I came out my mother's womb valuable!

Then proceed (in my Lil Kim voice) to start bumping Kendrick Lamar "I love myself" song," do the walk he did in the video and everything. Fe-Fi-Fo-Fum.

MARRIED WOMEN

VS

SINGLE WOMEN

THE SET UP

I feel that a lot of 20th century concepts are being used in the 21st century. I feel the needs of the 21st century woman is different than the women of the 20th century.

I had an associate who grew up in the Deep South. She would always tell me that a woman should do everything in her power not to allow a guy to get access to her honey (another word for vagina). She would say that she was taught that once a guy had gotten the "honey" he had nothing else to work for. The guy should have to *work* for the honey. I see this thought process all the time. This concept is also given as advice. I heard this comment so often that it made me start to ask questions, like: "Why deal with someone who only wants one thing from you?" and "Is there not more to a woman than her 'honey'?"

The Observations of DaSh'e

Unfortunately, the asking of these questions came with rebuke 101. Such as, how dare "I" a "single" woman dare question a "married woman?" She was a "wife" and I was "single." So, I'm supposed to just listen to her advice? See the hook?

Third perspective: I think that for women who were taught this type of thought process, it possibly came from dealing with males who were the breadwinners and who had control over the finances. In this type of scenario, the woman doesn't have control of the finances, but she did have her "honey." So, I feel that this created a type of barter type system. In some ways, if the advice had come across more balanced versus "you listen to me because Izza married, and I have the key (think of the opening to He-Man cartoon.). I think I could have taken it from a more balanced approach, such as allow a man to give to you. Allow yourself to receive – especially coming from a background that a woman is to be independent.

The Discussion

1. Do you feel that there is a hierarchy when it comes to women?

   _____

   _____

   _____

   _____

   _____

2. If so do you feel that this hierarchy leads to competitiveness?

_____

_____

_____

_____

_____

3. Have you ever been given romantic advice that just didn't resonate with you?

_____

_____

_____

_____

_____

4. Did you ever feel out of the "loop" when it came to how to "get a man"?

_____

_____

_____

_____

_____

_____

5. Do you feel that when we (female collective) address the competitiveness, we eventually will be able to learn from one another (divine feminine)?

_____

_____

_____

_____

_____

6. What is your suggestion?

_____

_____

_____

_____

_____

Mantra:

I surround myself with women who are for my highest good.

Sidebar from DaSh'e:

I feel that romantic advice is really just an individual's romantic preferences. A lot of times I hear people complain about how sistas are too independent. I never hear society get to the core of why, though. I would like to provide some insight from my personal experience. It was passed down to make you have your own, so you don't have to depend on a man. It was not told the reasons why. In hindsight, I think there were female relatives who were abused by males in the family, as well as their husbands. There is still this code that is passed down to protect or hold down these abusive guys in the family, no matter what – even if it involves sexual abuse. So, instead of the whole story being told, it was passed down to be an independent woman. Don't depend on a man. Case closed.

How do we address this behavior?

1. Stop with the hierarchy of women.

2. If hierarchy stops, competitiveness stops. Once competitiveness stops, understanding and compassion begin.

3. Once compassion begins learning begins.

4. From a balanced perspective, the "honey" sista could have learned that there is more to a woman than her vagina. There is no need for manipulation tactics that must be used to "catch" a man, like you're in a rodeo. It's okay to just be.

5. The "independent" sista could have learned from the "honey" sista that it is okay to allow herself to "receive." It's okay to ask questions. Don't allow herself to be shut down with asking questions. Questions bring understanding when their intent is to gain understanding and not to have a "battle of the wits."

TEAM MAKEUP
VS
TEAM NO MAKEUP

THE SET UP

I've had personal a situation in which I must say I love makeup! I love how it makes me feel. I love the art of it. I love the feel of cotton (just playing). Seriously though, I love it. I also love to dance. I would frequent the local Zumba classes in the area. I loved the Zumba classes, because they showed me how to connect to my Divine Feminine nature in a safe place, or so I thought. It was at this time when I encountered individuals who would ask me why I would wear makeup to Zumba class. My question back would be, *why not*? It's not as though my day started with Zumba — especially with the class being held at night. Boy, did that open up a can of worms. The random comments were things such as, "my husband told me the reason why he loves me so much is because I don't put all that crap on my face." To me, I'm sure that there were other reasons why he loved her, but I just really thought that was a really "random" thing to say. In hindsight, it's laughable, and I must learn that some people love to try to find a person's weakness, because they feel weak inside.

THE HOOK

1. Shaming of how another woman chooses to adorn her body. This is another competitive category used to divide women.

2. Another hierarchy example: women who wear makeup are trying to hide.

3. Women who are "natural" are lazy and refuse to put forth effort concerning their physical appearance.

How do we address this behavior?

1. Appreciate the diversity of beauty when it comes to women.

2. Compliment. Compliments can cure jealousy. They can also curb competition. By giving another woman a compliment, you are telling a woman what you admire about her, and it can make her day brighter. Honestly, a lot of times the compliment of what they admire about you is given. So, it's a win-win :).

3. When males who do not have an interest in healing women for the better make comments, address those comments right then and there. I've even had situations in which I've asked the question: "out of all the shit going on in the world, why are you worried about how a woman chooses to adorn herself?"

The Discussion

1. Have you ever been shamed for how you chose to adorn your body?

_____

_____

_____

_____

_____

2. Do you feel that there is competitiveness between women? If so, in what areas?

_____

_____

_____

_____

_____

3. Have you ever encountered a male who has a platform geared toward women; however, the advice did not resonate?

_____

_____

_____

_____

_____

4. How did it make you feel?

_____

_____

_____

_____

_____

5. What are your views on males who have platforms geared toward women?

_____

_____

_____

_____

_____

_____

6. Do you feel that there are males who have platforms geared toward women with ulterior motives to have sexual encounters with women? If so who?

_____

_____

_____

_____

_____

7. What are your suggestions on how to deal with these types of males with ulterior motives?

_____

_____

_____

_____

_____

_____

Mantra:

Beauty is not owned.

WOMEN WITH KIDS
VS.
WOMEN WITHOUT KIDS

THE SET UP

I've been asked by people on multiple occasions if I have children. For me, it seems as another way to divide women. For some women including myself, the question has been asked. Why? What's wrong with you? You better hurry up and have some! With some males, I have been accused of being a "selfish" woman. I have also been told I'm not a real woman yet (lol). As if.

I've talked to some women who do have children and some of the shaming tactics that have been said to them have been atrocious as well. Especially the ignorant statement such as "ain't no man gone want you." Which is a lie.

THE HOOK

1. This is yet another way to divide women into "more of a woman"/"less of a woman."

2. Society has a way of automatically putting women in the "bad mother" category. Example: when a woman wants time to herself, she's a bad mother.

3. This type of mentality causes some women to feel as if they cannot openly talk about or vent about what they deal with as mothers. This in turn causes some to put this anger on to women who have no kids or to utilize the shaming tactics that have been placed on them.

4. Some women see the unfair treatment toward mothers in society and choose not to have children.

5. Some women who don't have children throw the fact that they don't have kids into women who do have children's faces.

6. Some women who have children will do or say things to antagonize women with no kids such as, "girl yo' eggs gone dry up." In some instances, the way they say it actually sound like they frying eggs.

The Observations of DaSh'e

1. Recognize the hook.

2. Women who don't have children could learn another aspect to the art of multi-tasking from women with children. Women who have no children could teach women who have children to relax and that it is okay to take time for self.

3. Women who have children could ask for women who

don't have children to babysit for them from time to time. Women who don't have children could learn the art of being in the present moment from children.

4. Appreciate each other. Realize we all have our own journeys, paths, and lessons to learn.

The Discussion

1. Have you ever had a situation in which individuals were a little bit too concerned about your uterus?

_____

_____

_____

_____

_____

_____

2. Have you ever been overly concerned with another woman's uterus? If so why?

_____

_____

_____

_____

_____

_____

3. Do you feel that society puts mothers in the "bad mother" category too quickly?

_____

_____

_____

_____

_____

4. Do you feel society pressures women into motherhood? If so, in what ways?

_____

_____

_____

_____

_____

5. Have you ever had a "team kids" vs. "team no kids" experience?

_____

_____

_____

_____

_____

_____

6. How did it make you feel?

_____

_____

_____

_____

_____

7. What are your suggestions?

_____

_____

_____

_____

_____

Random Thoughts from DaSh'e

I've always wondered why society uses shaming techniques on women such as, "Girl you better hurry up and have some kids before your eggs dry up!" They act like a woman's eggs are like that old school 1980's commercial "This is your brain on drugs."

Mantra:

I am not my eggs (in my India Arie voice -- just joking).

Mantra:

I define what works for me.

MANIPULATIVE TACTICS TO TRY TO GET SISTAS TO CONFORM. FOR WHAT? THERE IS NO BENEFIT.

THE SET UP

A few years ago, I was taking classes at a local massage school in the Virginia Beach, VA area – specifically the Edgar Cayce Massage Therapy School. Remember the ready-made box? I soon realized the issue wasn't me per se. However, the media portrays sistas in a certain way, and individuals don't critically think about television programming. They tend to go with the narrative. It's kinda a trip, though, while being in a classroom setting. If I speak loudly, I'm being "aggressive" or either the new buzz word for ghetto: *raaaaaccccchettt*. If I'm quiet, I have an "attitude." **SEE THE HOOK?** I realized very quickly it was not my job to tap dance for these individuals in an attempt to make them comfortable. The uncomfortableness that they were dealing with was within themselves. Not me.

THE HOOK

A lot of times, it seems that some white women have a type of fear factor or uncomfortableness and instead of addressing it within themselves it seems all too easy for them to push the responsibility onto sistas. I like to call it the "sista panic alert button." In a lot of ways, it seems as if sistas are an easier target, because it's easier for white women to play double dutch by throwing attacks and then jump behind the rope of protection. "I'm scared. Help me." If the sista chooses to take the responsibility for their "uncomfortableness," there is a chance she (the sista) begins to feel uncomfortable if not already. How, you may ask?

Well, some sistas are made to feel there is something wrong with them, so they (the sistas) need to do something to make the white women feel comfortable. Example: Talking in a "softer" tone. Making jokes. Smiling more. Even if the sista is just naturally like this, for some people just by bringing this subject up is uncomfortable. My response is when honesty is not brought forth, this creates an imbalance because the sista is forced into a "performance" role to accommodate this white woman's feelings of inadequacies.

The fact of the matter is it wasn't even the sistas' inadequacies that were coming to the forefront. It was the white woman's inadequacies that were coming forth. However, if we go with the narrative that is portrayed, these types of white women don't want the secret to come out. Because that would knock them off of the top of the so-called hierarchy chain. Let's be real; if you have "OMG! FLAWS," you can no longer be under the false illusion anymore of being the epitome of beauty.

The Observations of DaSh'e

How do we address this behavior?

1. White women with this type of mindset: be open and honest about how you feel. But also, be open to the suggestions on how to deal with your insecurities ON YOUR OWN.

2. White women stand on your OWN two feet without trying to use sistas as a scapegoat.

3. Sistas: let these types of white women with this type of mindset know that their behavior will not be tolerated at your expense.

4. Sistas: recognize the trigger words for exactly what they are — triggers designed to get you triggered. You don't have to take on those words into your inner being.

The Discussion

1. Have you ever experienced a competitive/ignorant situation in an academic setting?

_____

_____

_____

_____

_____

2. How did you handle it?

_____

_____

_____

_____

_____

_____

3. Were there trigger words used?

_____

_____

_____

_____

_____

4. What are some of the steps you think the academic world can take to combat this type of mentality in a class room setting?

_____

_____

_____

_____

_____

5. Do you feel that sistas get used as scapegoats sometimes? If so how? How does this make you feel?

_____

_____

_____

_____

_____

_____

6. What are your interlude/suggestions to deal with this issue?

_____

_____

_____

_____

_____

_____

Mantra:

I speak my truth!

TRYING TO PUT DIRT ON SISTAS TO MAKE YOU LOOK TALLER

THE SET UP

I was watching a Roland Martin show. On this particular show, they had Dr. Umar Johnson who had made comments on a radio show. There were three other individuals on the panel. My particular issue with this lecturer was that before he even got to the crux of his issue, he threw out all of these unbalanced statistics aka "scare tactics" concerning sistas and how they are the least to get married, etc. Where does this dynamic come in that in order to talk about issues within the so-called black community, you must first throw dirt on sistas? How is this dirt thrown?

The Observations of DaSh'e

1. Spitting out unbalanced statistics aka scare tactics, e.g, sistas are the least likely to get married. Remember, they like to try to equate this with a sistas worth.

2. The stomping on or shaming of sistas that are single mothers. In some instances, this tactic is also used as

a way to manipulate single mothers for selfish use of their vaginas.

3. Using derogatory terms used to mask deep resentments towards sistas, e.g, "bed wench."

4. My question is this: is the sista a bed wench, or is it that she is just exploring her sexuality?

5. This seems like a herd type of mentality where if you make sistas feel that they have no options, it keeps them fenced in. It almost seems as though it's a selfish manipulation tactic that is used like a sista trying to play duck-duck goose and is supposed to be excited because she got chosen. The signs of this duck- duck goose mentality to me surfaces as:

   • Any rhetoric that starts out saying sistas are the "least to" or "8 out 10 black women are...."

   • This rhetoric includes S.T.D. statistics as H.I.V. statistics. This includes pictures that are subliminally put in place along with the news article, which imply a lot. Remember, we are dealing with an imbalance, so when statistics are put out there about an alarming H.I.V. rate concerning sistas (and then a subliminally big-ass picture with an innocent sista simply getting her blood drawn in the hospital probably there to just get a regular health check up), it alludes to a lot of things.

Let's be honest; there is still a lot of stigma surrounding H.I.V. It's gotten to the point where not only are the statistics attacking sistas for their outside appearance but now they are also attacking sistas internally as well by putting false statistics concerning sistas' internal health.

How do we address this behavior?

1. If an individual does not have the intention of trying to heal a sista, they need to stay out of a sista's issues.

2. If an individual is trying to heal sistas, do it with pure motives.

3. We, as a society, need to call out individuals' behavior the moment they begin to throw dirt on sistas.

4. Individuals who throw dirt on sistas need to be asked "why?" -- by themselves, as well as others.

5. When a sista calls out these individuals' behavior, don't use manipulation tactics to try to shut them down.

6. For those this applies to, ask yourself what type of gratification you get from throwing dirt on sistas.

7. We should acknowledge the efforts that single mothers make to run a household.

8. Provide a safe haven where single mothers or mothers in general can really voice the things that they deal with without being thrown in the "bad mother category."

The Discussion: Statistic or Static?

1. Do you feel that the statistics are balanced when it comes to sistas?

   _____

   _____

   _____

   _____

   _____

2. Do you feel the term "single mother" is used as a shaming tactic?

   _____

   _____

   _____

   _____

   _____

3. Are there other terms you feel are used to shame sistas? If so, what are those terms? How do they make you feel?

   _____

   _____

   _____

   _____

   _____

4. What are some of the manipulation tactics that you feel are used to keep sistas boxed in?

_____

_____

_____

_____

_____

_____

5. How does it make you feel?

_____

_____

_____

_____

_____

_____

6. Do you feel that these same manipulation tactics are used to toward women of other nationalities?

_____

_____

_____

_____

_____

7. If so, why do you think this is so?

_____

_____

_____

_____

_____

8. Do you feel that other women of other nationalities deal with manipulation tactics as well but just a different form? If so why?

_____

_____

_____

_____

_____

9. Do you feel that women of other nationalities contribute to these manipulation tactics? If so why?

_____

_____

_____

_____

_____

10. Do you feel that manipulation tactics plays into how sista's and women of other nationalities interact with one another? If so, how?

_____

_____

_____

_____

_____

11. Do you feel that manipulation tactics play into how sistas and women of other nationalities interact with one another? If so, how?

_____

_____

_____

_____

_____

12. What are some Interlude or suggestions do you have to help bring balance to the female collective to heal as a whole?

_____

_____

_____

_____

Mantra:

I define my worth.

THE DIFFERENCE BETWEEN FAMILY AND PEOPLE YOU ARE JUST RELATED TO

THE SET UP

Sometimes sadly before the media gets to some sistas, the hook can even come from relatives.

THE HOOK

The hook can come in different forms: the look of your facial features, the look of your hair texture, the length of your hair, as well as what your "status" is going to be in life.

Sidebar by DaSh'e

1. This is sad, because I feel that family is a starter foundation and our precious sistas are the home. A strong foundation is put forth and filled with love with words of empowerment, words of affirmation, and telling sistas what they are good at. That way, when the storms of the media and what other people say come, it doesn't matter because sistas know that they were built on a firm foundation.

2. It is reasons such as the above why I can understand why some sistas refuse to go back home, even if it is to visit. You also have some sistas who, if they do have to

go back home, it's a cap of three days maximum.

3. Shaming tactics as well as manipulation tactics used such as: you don't come back because you to "gooooood" now. You gotta make sure to pronounce all the "o's."

4. You forgot where you "came from."

5. Vicious rumors will be circulated that can take you for a loop. A lot of times, I've noticed that the vicious rumors are a tactic used if relatives feel that they can't piece your life together. This tactic is especially used if you don't discuss your personal business with certain relatives.

6. A discord between the generations.

7. Even though some sistas are in their 20's, 30's, 40's and beyond, (I know it sounds star-trekish, but flow with me for a second), there are some sistas who still walk around with the hurt and pain they experienced during childhood. Some psychologists call it the "inner child."

I'm learning that it is not possible to heal in the same environment in which I got sick. A lot of times, I wish that relatives would understand or at least look at the perspective that it is really about self-preservation. With certain types of relatives, no matter what you do it's never good enough. You could be the President of the United States, and they're going to say "well, she ain't the President of the Universe!" You could then decide to become the President of Galaxy, then they'd say "well, she ain't the President of Infinity!" See what I mean, sis? Sis, just leave 'em be. (You can't see it, but I'm sitting here shaking my head.)

The Observations of DaSh'e

<u>How do we address this behavior?</u>

1. For the older generation, STOP competing and projecting YOUR insecurities onto the next generation.

2. For the older generation, live YOUR dreams, live YOUR best life, because once you do, you won't have to compare -- which leads to competing with the next generation.

3. Compliment. I'm talking about a sincere high vibration compliment. Not one of those back handed compliments. "Girrrrrrrl, you sho' did grow into your face. (Yes, this has happened.) In my opinion, one of the best cures for jealousy/envy is to compliment the person you are jealous or envious of. It's a win-win situation. They feel better from the compliment, and you feel better because you are no longer harboring jealous/envious energy inside your body.

4. Know the difference between relatives and family. In my opinion, family is a basic unit of people who love and support you and who want the best for you. Relatives are just people who you are related to.

The Discussion

1. Did you come from a family that you felt empowered you?

_____

_____

_____

_____

_____

2. If so, in what ways did it make you feel empowered?

_____

_____

_____

_____

_____

3. Did you have to deal with relatives who you felt disempowered you? In what ways?

_____

_____

_____

_____

_____

_____

4. Does it still affect you? If so, how?

_____

_____

_____

_____

_____

5. Do you feel that relatives made a difference in how they treated the boys in the family? In what ways?

_____

_____

_____

_____

_____

6. How did it make you feel? In what ways?

_____

_____

_____

_____

_____

7. Does it still affect you?

_____

_____

_____

_____

_____

8. Have you been able to openly talk about it?

_____

_____

_____

_____

_____

9. Does it feel odd to you when you see women who are supported by their family?

_____

_____

_____

_____

10. Do you feel that when women are supported by their family that they are being babied?

_____

_____

_____

_____

_____

11. Do you feel that there is an age limit to when sistas should not be supported by their families, financial or otherwise? Why?

_____

_____

_____

_____

_____

12. If so, is it because it's a sista? Is this same reasoning/ mentality applied towards other cultures? Subconsciously? Why or why not?

_____

_____

_____

_____

_____

13. If you have moved away from your hometown, would you go back? Why or why not?

_____

_____

_____

_____

_____

14. If you have not moved away, are you jealous of those who have moved away? Why or why not?

_____

_____

_____

_____

_____

15. Why do you feel there is a divide between some of the older and younger generation of women?

_____

_____

_____

_____

_____

16. What interlude/suggestions do you have to address these issues?

_____

_____

_____

_____

_____

Sidebar by DaSh'e:

For questions 14-16, it was brought about because I remember on Season 6 of "The Real Housewives of Atlanta," Porsha had moved in with her mother as she went through her divorce. I felt that it was wonderful to see Porsha being supported while going through her transition. However, I did notice that Porsha was being ridiculed for moving in with her mom. This made me question if this was because she was a "sista." To me, this was yet another unwritten rule that had been placed in the Sista Bible (Basic Instruction Book for Living on Earth) the T.T.K.S.D. (Tryin to Keep A Sista Down) version. It's a new cycle ladies, we are learning to live our best lives! We don't have time to go back and forth with these_____ (you fill in the blank).

Sista Watch for the Hook, Even in R&B

I felt that it was important to break this down into a musical piece (thanks Kanise). Believe it or not, music is influential (in-flow in to you) and has a way of influencing society, even if it is subtle. I'm not sure if you noticed, but I think it even can influence the way a woman is treated sexually. I rarely hear loving romantic terms nowadays when it comes to music. Nowadays when it comes to music, it's beating the puss-say, hitting the puss-say, tearing the puss-say up, even riding the puss-say like a stroller. Like WTF? Heck, next they gone be talking about torpedoing the pussy, yoni, pearl or whatever you choose to call your "sexual garden." In a weird way, it does feel like they have declared "war" on the puss-say.

For maximum effect, when saying the word puss-say, you gotta make sure you purse your lips together (pun intended), really pronounce the "p," and say it like you just ran out of breath when it comes to the "say" part. If you want to get real creative, you can pronounce it like Bernie Mac would: puuuuh -sayyyyyyyyy...

But I digress.

Now, I get it that there are people who have different tastes of music and at times are just committed to misunderstanding, especially when it comes to books like mine; however, I recognize also that there are people who might be wondering: well, DaSh'e: what's your intention? Well first, thank you for asking. Second, I want you to know that my intention is not to provoke discord. My intention is to provoke thought, which provokes conversation, which then opens the gates for healing to take place. That is, for those who are willing to walk through the gates.

I would also like to leave you with this final quote:

All truth passes through three stages.

First, it is ridiculed.

Second, it is violently opposed.

Third, it is accepted as being self-evident.

It's sad to say it has even seeped over into the R&B genre. It's like they done started mixing love songs with shade. At the time I am writing this piece, a popular song on the radio is "When We" by Tank. Isn't it ironic that his name is Tank? Remember the torpedoes.

Now Sista - Watch for The Hook.

> *Who came to make sweet love? Not me*
>
> *Who came to kiss and hug? Not me*
>
> *Who came to beat it up? Rocky*
>
> *And don't use those hands to put up that gate and*
>
> *stop me*

> *[insert Scooby-doo sound]*

It's interesting that the character from *Rocky* was used, because in my mind, I can imagine some dudes literally in the freezer like: Rocky was "beating the puss-ssay up" gray sweatsuit and all -- sweating and grunting, just angry. Not me.

On a serious note, that last lyric is a little disturbing to say the least, but hey: it's just a "song" right? The other part of the song that was a little Scooby-Doo for me was in the re-mix. Now, I will admit the remix alluded slightly to love-making but it took a turn on this verse:

> *You got plenty miles and baggage*
> *But I could still make you a savage*

[Double Scooby doo on THIS one.]

This has been the FIRST R&B "love song" that I have heard, and it was mixed with some shade. For y'all seasoned folks/old heads or whatever you want to call it, do you remember the time if men couldn't express their admiration for you in words, they would take the lyrics from the back of a c.d. cover and serenade you or write it in a card and give it to you -- sometimes with a rose attached?

Issssssssssssssssssssssssssh. Not nowadays.

These R&B lyrics will almost get you cut or shot depending on who you are dealing with. I wish a dude would tell me when we about to make love, "Now, gyyyrl, I know you got 'plenty' of miles and baggage." Matter of fact, he wouldn't be able to make it to the second verse. (I'm just playing Universe, gotta be mindful what you wish for.)

I think for me, the other issue is too many songs that are talking about f****** a woman and not enough songs talking about making love to a woman. And, yes, there is a diffrence.

Let's bring back the essence of making love and caressing each other. I'm about to go in my Lisa McDowell voice mode (*Coming to America*) when she was in the auditorium speaking at the "Black Awareness Rally" asking for donations.

Here is my version: *We are NOT happy to get the dicks that mingle, but we would rather get the dicks that jingle and know how to make love. Thank you.*

[Feel free to insert the word "wands." The right ones can be very magical.]

Mantra:

I surround myself with people and environments that are healthy and healing to my soul.

WHAT EXACTLY IS "BLACK CULTURE," AND WHAT IS THE "DESIGNATED SPACE?"

THE SET UP

These past couple of months leading up to the publication of this book have been eye-opening to the point that I felt it was imperative to ask two questions: 1) What exactly is so-called Black Culture? 2) What is this designated place that so-called black people are supposed to be in? First things first, let's tackle the first question.

What exactly is Black Culture?

In my personal observation, I feel that the problem is that society tries to place black culture in a Little Caesar's Hot-N-Ready box.

What's inside? Hmmmmm let's take a peek.

The Observations of DaSh'e

To me, the deeper issue is that society tries to box so-called black culture under the guise of "hood." In my opinion, "hood" is not connected to skin color, but it is connected to an

SISTA, WATCH FOR THE HOOK!

individual's mentality. I think that people fail to realize that there are so many different aspects, as well as subcultures in the melanated community. Here is the list that I have come up with so far.

1. College Culture: those who have attended and are in college

2. Sorority and Fraternity Culture: those who pledged into sororities and fraternities

3. Church Culture: those who attend church and rep they churches like they are in an actual sorority or fraternity. C.O.G.I.C. (stand up), shoot, just attending ONE of y'all long church services feels like an initiation.

4. Hip Hop/Rap Culture: those who listen to hip-hop/rap and can tell you the difference between the two.

5. Spiritual Culture: those who are on their own spiritual path and recognize the spiritual nature of life and how it's all connected

6. Conscious Culture: those who are aware of the different levels of situations.

7. Tech Culture: those who are into computers and the inner workings of technology.

8. Book Culture: those who enjoy books and sometimes join book clubs to discuss different aspects

9. Food Culture: those who enjoy food and the different texture of food. My personal favorite aspect of food culture is to hear a brotha talk about ribs. I do not know

what it is about a man in his 40's and above and the way they talk about ribs, but it's quite entertaining. They be like, "sooooo..." They voice get real deep (the song "I'd Rather Be With You" by Bootsie Collins starts playing in the background.). They be like, you take the ribs and you rub 'em down. You make sure that you rub EVERY inch. Make sure you take your time now (in my Bootsie Collins' voice), then you have the sauce -- the meat be falling off the bone. Just tender. The brothas lips start watering and shit, and it's at this point where you have to step in and ask if they are talking about rib tips or a woman. By the way, does anybody remember G. Garvin?

10. Metaphysical Culture: those who enjoy the philosophy of nature and discussing the different aspects of reality

11. Military Culture: those who have had dealings in the military through the various branches of the armed forces

12. Athletic Fitness Culture: those who enjoy the working out of their bodies and the transformation process

These are just a couple of the cultures that I have come up with. I'm sure that there are many more. To me, this just shows that there is more to see. There are many different aspects of the melanated culture/community than the ready-made box.

You may ask what "Well, what is wrong with the ready-made box? It's too restricted, and it allows no room for growth.

Now on to the second question.

What is the issue with this "designated place" that so-called "black people" are supposed to be in? My issue with this "designated place" is that it is disempowering and serves no benefits to the melanated community — especially the melanated woman.

To be honest, I can understand why the so-called "bougie" or "middle class" black people have created their own subculture amongst themselves. Imagine wanting and having the things that you desire and deserve in life only to be told by certain white people that you shouldn't have these things. Then, you find that these comments are made as well by people who have the same complexion as you. This is not healthy or balanced. It is enough to make anyone feel alienated. That, my friends, is not okay.

To be quite honest, this is one of my questions to society: who or what designated this belief system that only "white people" are to have nice things or to live a life of luxury?

What's even more sad is it can be passed down. I've had an older woman try to shame me by saying that the difference between me and her is that she was raised "not to show everything she got" (material things, as well as her nice clothes). I told her that doesn't sound beneficial or empowering; in fact, it sounds very disempowering.

I'm at a point in my life where I feel if it's disempowering to my psyche, I'm releasing it. I've come to the conclusion that cowering down to make someone feel comfortable is not beneficial or healthy. I CHOOSE HEALTH, and I CHOOSE SELF-PRESERVATION. To do this is important because, sistas, we have purpose on this earth plane, and it is up to us to fulfill our purpose.

The Discussion

Questions for Society

1. Do you feel that you try to categorize the so-called Black Community? In what ways?

_____

_____

_____

_____

_____

2. Why do you feel that you don't do this categorization when it comes to your OWN culture or race?

_____

_____

_____

_____

_____

3. Growing up, what were you taught about the so-called Black Community?

_____

_____

_____

_____

_____

4. Do you feel that this is fair? Why or why not?

_____

_____

_____

_____

_____

_____

5. Does it bother you to see other races or nationalities prosper? Why or why not?

_____

_____

_____

_____

_____

_____

6. What are some suggestions that you have to address this?

_____

_____

_____

_____

_____

Questions for the Melanated Community

1. Were you ever taught that because you were melanated you shouldn't have certain things? Why or why not?

_____

_____

_____

_____

_____

2. How did it make you feel?

_____

_____

_____

_____

_____

3. Do you feel this type of teaching was beneficial? If not, in what ways have you decided to combat this mindset?

_____

_____

_____

_____

_____

4. What are your solutions/suggestions?

_____

_____

_____

_____

_____

SO, I LEAVE YOU WITH THIS:
THE IMPORTANCE OF WRITING ABOUT THE INSECURE WHITE WOMAN

I feel that in order to truly experience AUTHENTIC women empowerment, as well as connecting to the divine feminine consciousness, we have to address some of the underlying issues.

At this point it feels like a lot of issues are coming up. The issues are like lava erupting out of the top of a volcano. You have some individuals who choose to try to subdue the lava even attempting to sit on top of the volcano hoping that the lava won't come to the surface. You have some individuals who are embracing the lava and steam knowing that the lava represents the underlying emotions that have been wanting to come to the surface. Through addressing some of these underlying issues within the feminine collective, we can see the divide and conquer techniques that are used by the unbalanced patriarchal mindset, which relies heavily on creating competition between women.

Examples of this type of competition are the following:

1. Conducting studies of which race is deemed more attractive than others. Yes, they definitely "study" to do studies to figure out what to do next.

2. Telling one race of women why they are better than another; however, dabbling with both races, they are trying to pit one against another for selfish motives.

3. Perpetuating the false propaganda that there are not enough males.

4. Perpetuating that one race of females is more likely to contract sexual diseases than another race or nationality of women.

5. When it comes to a certain race of males, particularly black males, that there are not enough. Some even go so far as to say there aren't enough GOOD, black males. So, you have to take what you can get. Due to this propaganda, they started coming out with books on "How to Get A Man." Like women are some damn farmers trying to catch some damn chickens in a chicken coop. The chicken doing football moves and spins on you and isssh (just joking).

6. The propaganda that there are more women on the planet than men.

7. Trying to create a hierarchy when it comes to categorizing women, wives, girlfriends, and single women, as well as other titles.

All in all, a lot of this seems as though there is competition amongst some of the males and some of them are trying to use women as collateral. We have a choice in the matter. I must admit; some of us as women have played right into it. One of the solutions is to first deal with these matters within ourselves.

The second is to deal with these matters amongst ourselves. I get that for some individuals, no matter what you do, they are committed to misunderstanding you.

Disclaimer: For those types, this book, as well as my articles, are not for you.

I realize that for healing to take place, sometimes there have to be uncomfortable conversations, but through these conversations can come healing. For those who choose to take that path, we can do this!

It's time.

Dipped in Love,

DaSh'e

Activate Highest Good Only

AFTERWORD

Cue in the intro to Queen Latifah's "U.N.I.T.Y." Yes, I do have my camel-skin hoodie on as I write this, but I digress. All in all sistas, I just want you to know that "You Got the Power." I know at times it get's kinda heavy and makes you wanna S.N.A.P (pun intended) but you know sis, like "Glenda the Good Witch" says, "you had the power all along my dear." So, let's RE-introduce ourselves...

Activate Highest Good Only,

DaSh'e

www.ingramcontent.com/pod-product-compliance
Lightning Source LLC
LaVergne TN
LVHW011411080426
835511LV00005B/480